Do Frogs Drink Hot Chocolate?

How Animals Keep Warm

With warmth, for my darling Benjamin—E.K.   Thank you, LDA—J.M.

Thank you to editor Jennifer MacKinnon for her insight, creativity, and good humor; to John Martz for his lovable, laugh-out-loud illustrations; and to designers Danielle Arbour and Alisa Baldwin for their clever design.—Etta Kaner

Text © 2018 Etta Kaner
Illustrations © 2018 John Martz

Owlkids Books acknowledges the financial support of the Canada Council for the Arts, the Ontario Arts Council, the Government of Canada through the Canada Book Fund (CBF) and the Government of Ontario through the Ontario Media Development Corporation's Book Initiative for our publishing activities.

Published in Canada by
Owlkids Books Inc.
10 Lower Spadina Avenue
Toronto, ON M5V 2Z2

Published in the United States by
Owlkids Books Inc.
1700 Fourth Street
Berkeley, CA 94710

Library and Archives Canada Cataloguing in Publication

Kaner, Etta, author
    Do frogs drink hot chocolate? : how animals keep warm / written by Etta Kaner ; illustrated by John Martz.

ISBN 978-1-77147-292-0 (hardcover)

    1. Body temperature--Regulation--Juvenile literature. 2. Animal heat-- Juvenile literature. I. Martz, John, 1978-, illustrator II. Title.

QP135.K38 2018   j571.7'61   C2017-907265-X

Library of Congress Control Number: 2017917316

Edited by Jennifer MacKinnon
Designed by Danielle Arbour and Alisa Baldwin
The display typeface in this book is Manhattan Hand, courtesy of Noble People

Manufactured in Shenzhen, China, in March 2018, by C&C Joint Printing Co.
Job #HS0389

A   B   C   D   E   F

Publisher of Chirp, chickaDEE and OWL
www.owlkidsbooks.com

Owlkids Books is a division of

Bayard
CANADA

Do Frogs Drink Hot Chocolate?

How Animals Keep Warm

Written by **Etta Kaner**

Illustrated by **John Martz**

Owlkids Books

When it gets cold out, do animals turn up the heat?

So how do they survive
the chilly weather? Let's find out...

Do frogs drink hot chocolate to keep warm?

NO!

Some frogs don't even try to keep warm. The Alaskan wood frog turns into a frogsicle! It spends the winter with most of its body frozen. When the air warms up, the frog warms up, too.

Do penguins snuggle with a friend?

In winter, thousands of emperor penguins come together in a giant huddle. It's warm in the middle, but cold on the outside. So what do they do? The penguin shuffle! Taking small steps, they slowly change places. That way, they all get a turn in the middle.

Do butterflies sunbathe?

YES!

Butterflies can't fly if they are cold. And they can't make their own heat. So what do they do? Catch some rays! If it's cold, a butterfly will sit on a rock or log and stretch its wings. Then the sun warms up its flight muscles.

Do foxes wear earmuffs?

Arctic foxes have small, furry ears. The fur helps, but so does the size. Ears stick out into the cold air. A fox's body can lose heat that way. Smaller ears don't stick out as much as big ears, so they lose less heat.

Do turtles jump up and down to keep warm?

NO!

Many turtles will burrow into the mud and dead leaves at the bottom of a pond. The water there is cold, but it never freezes. It usually stays at about 39°F (3.8°C). That's the perfect temperature for turtles who like to snooze while they wait for spring!

Do polar bears build homes?

YES!

Pregnant polar bears build dens. But not with wood and hammers! Instead, a mama bear uses her sharp claws to dig out a cave in the snow. When it's finished, she crawls inside to have her babies. The den keeps them all safe and warm until spring.

Do whales wear snowsuits?

NO!

Whales have blubber under their skin. This layer of fat keeps their body heat in and the cold out. Whale blubber can be up to 12 inches (30 cm) thick! It also stores energy, so whales can keep going for a long time without eating.

Do squirrels curl up under blankets?

YES! (SORT OF)

Squirrels have built-in blankets. When it's cold out, they wrap their long, bushy tails around themselves so their body heat won't escape. And that's not all! As the temperature drops, less blood flows into their tails. Instead, it stays in their bodies to help keep them warm.

Do monkeys
take hot baths
to keep warm?

YES!

Japanese macaques love to take warm baths! There are places in Japan where hot water bubbles up naturally from the ground to form pools. After playing in the snow, the macaques will jump into these hot pools to warm up.

Do tuataras sit by a campfire?

NO!

Tuataras' bodies cannot make heat. But birds' bodies can. So what does a tuatara do? It has a sleepover with a little bird called a fairy prion. The heat from the bird helps keep the tuatara from getting too chilly overnight.

Do honeybees use teamwork?

YES!

In the winter, honeybees form a cluster around the queen bee. Then they shiver together. By vibrating their wing muscles, they raise the air temperature in the hive. This keeps the queen toasty warm. How do bees have energy for all this shivering? They eat honey!

Do birds fly south?

In winter, some birds fly south in search of food and warmth. Other birds survive wintry weather by eating as much as possible. This gives their bodies energy to keep warm. Feathers help, too. When they're fluffed up, they trap warm air next to a bird's skin.

Do guanacos wear leg warmers to keep warm?

YES! (SORT OF)

Guanacos have thick, woolly coats. But there is very little fur on their legs. When it's cold outside, chilly guanacos lie down with their legs tucked under their bodies. That keeps them nice and warm.

All of the animals in this book have special ways to survive the cold.

But what about you?
What do YOU do to keep warm?